Waiting for Rain

poems by

Mary Fox

Finishing Line Press
Georgetown, Kentucky

Waiting for Rain

Copyright © 2016 by Mary Fox
ISBN 978-1-63534-034-1 First Edition
All rights reserved under International and Pan-American Copyright Conventions.
No part of this book may be reproduced in any manner whatsoever without written permission from the publisher, except in the case of brief quotations embodied in critical articles and reviews.

ACKNOWLEDGMENTS

"Winter's Last Day" *River Poets Journal 2014*

I would like to thank Rosalie Sanara Petrouske, for aiding me in the editing and preparation of my manuscript, and my fellow Writing at the Ledges members who mentored and supported my writing.

Publisher: Leah Maines

Editor: Christen Kincaid

Cover Art: "Girl with Dandelion" by Arlene Bragg

Author Photo: Rosalie Sanara Petrouske

Cover Design: Elizabeth Maines

Printed in the USA on acid-free paper.
Order online: www.finishinglinepress.com
also available on amazon.com

Author inquiries and mail orders:
Finishing Line Press
P. O. Box 1626
Georgetown, Kentucky 40324
U. S. A.

Table of Contents

Summer's Eve, Waiting for Rain 1

Break-fast 2

Openings 3

Living in Limbo 4

The Garden Edge 6

Snow Angel 7

Blue-black Chair 8

The Gift of Pause 10

Winter's Last Day 11

Glitter 12

Graveyard Melodies 14

River Ride 15

Kitties Kiss 16

Deliberate Blindness 17

Grandma's Icebox 18

Night Lights 20

Clive's Magic 21

Some Dreams 22

In Dreams 23

I Didn't Get the Joke 24

Dregs of Winter 25

In loving memory of my mother, Hettie Williams Scully, whose wisdom and love guided me all my life.

Summer's Eve, Waiting for Rain

Sometimes on a summer's
eve, you can hear the thunder's
rumble creeping in, but you still gaze
at a star-studded sky hung with a sliver
of white-pie moon.
Under that canopy, you inhale
deeply the moist, worm-scented,
air. Rain will come;
you might feel it
in the stillness or in the warm
dampness of a clinging
shirt. You might even see
it in distant flashes backlighting
the yard, but there, by the deck,
in the glow
spilling from the kitchen
window, the leaves are green
and the flowers poise
for sleep, serene and lovely.

Break-fast

I could not swallow
the tone of your voice
when it appeared over oatmeal,
tart and venomous.

Throughout the day, I held
back the bile, rising in gut-wrenching
tides and swamping the lowlands
where hope clung,
until it became
anger-logged then empty.

As afternoon waned
I knew I could never ingest
what you offered.
I packed your bags
and left them on the porch
beside an empty bowl.

Openings

If I pulled open a curtain,
    I might notice the cats
    have squabbled in the long shadows
    opening to morning, cracking flower pots
    and spilling moist soil on oiled deck planks.
If I opened the curtains,
    my neighbors might see the spill of papers,
    orange juice on my dining room table,
    shoes dumped by the doorway,
    half-read magazines scattered on the couch.
    I might tidy the rooms.
If I pulled back a curtain,
    sunlight might puddle before my sliding doors
    bleaching the wood,
    defining pale edges of my life—
    its dark center hidden,
    cached beneath an indifferent rug.
If I opened up the curtain,
    I might fog my TV screen with daylight glare,
    blur messages,
    glowing dust twirling in rays,
    then in flickering spirals,
    rethink my days, my life, my purpose.
If I pulled open the curtains.

Living in Limbo

Lazyboy-ed,
stretched back,
feet propped,
his eyes droop in almost sleep.
He peers at an early evening rerun,
Gunsmoke—
dreamscape of "wish-it-were,"
he'd longed for as a boy—
when everything was black and white,
and the good guys hung out
with Matt and Kitty
at the Long Branch.
In "wish-it-were,"
men belly up to the bar
to settle problems,
solvable in half-hour segments,
with a little help from Doc
or Festus
or Chester.

Still, what is, and what will be,
floats around him
in the high plains of maybe,
and maybe not.
His hand brushes his now-short frizz,
crispy in a 1950s buzz cut.
Everywhere else he's lost hair,
emasculated.

Lassoed,
tied down in blue tubing
by a stranger who rolled in
to perch under a window
and stayed,
humming and whispering
"What's to come?"
in a monotonous lisp,

he waits for Doc to ride in
with a bag of tricks
to heal what ails him,
or for Kitty to find a brew
to mute it all.
But in his land,
Matt can't jail the monsters
or finagle them out of town
or out-shoot them in a gunfight,
and when he honestly lays down his cards
and looks out the swinging doors
to the orange light on the horizon,
nothing growing
is the best he hopes for.

The Garden Edge

November dampens
the morning air constricting my heart
at your empty garden's edge.

Snow Angel

One winter's morning, I leaned out
against the side door until it crunched
against the driveway's snowy ruts;
winter's blue whiteness,
in undulating drifts,
foamed to the backyard.
Dressed for play, I hesitated
to stamp my boots
in pristine snow that would
seep over my boot tops
and popsicle my toes. As I stood,
the crisp-air swirl provoked my mother
until she yelled "in or out!"
Startled, I leaped the driveway grooves
and ran bounding deer-like into backyard drifts,
twirling and spinning then tumbling
into the waves of snow.
I lay cocooned in frost, ready to transform.
I winged my arms and legs wildly
scraping the iciness beneath me
until minute snow balls grasped me,
their chilly hands pressed against the wooliness
of coat and gloves.

Awakened, I broke free,
whipping upright,
soaring like some exotic bird,
until I lighted at the driveway's frozen edge.
I grinned then turned to see
a perfect angel
shadowed in the snow.

Blue-black Chair

From my mother's room, I will save her bruised chair
where today she sits pulling pale stockings
over vein-stained legs.
Those legs carry her,
leaning on a walker, to her last days.

She moves more briskly than most anticipate,
so I tease her that she is training for races
we'll hold on her hundredth birthday.
In reality, I want her to slow down
and not speed too quickly to her end.

Still I know when she dies,
I will take that bruised chair home with me,
and its old black-and-blue print will clash
with the turquoise tranquility of my home.
I will find a place for it.

Later, when I miss her voice,
I will cloak myself in her chair,
conjuring her voice in reveries
and closing my eyes,
I will find her world imprinted
in its swirling pattern.

My mother would be surprised
I will take so much of her with me.
From the start, we pulled and pummeled each other.
My mother's daughter, more than my father's child,
I bear the curse of her intelligence,
will, and a too-giving heart
that carried all the worry of awareness—
its history fraught with poverty and death.

Once, I toddled across an unpaved street
to gather dandelions
growing in yellow empty-lot splendor.
Clutching their green-stemmed ooze,
I offered buttery tops to my mother.
She gathered my hands gently in hers
and conflicted, swatted my bottom
because I had ventured a road heedless
of potential dangers.
I felt the sting of rejection,
and we both wept.

My mother's life bloomed
in hillsides of disease, despair and death;
mine in the hot house of her love.
No, I will not weep for my mother.
I will know her.
A Persephone emerged from grief,
I will not spiral in sadness,
uncomforted in a world devoid
of Mother.
Cocooned in the shelter of her blue-black chair,
I will read the triumph of her life
and from the wisdom of her tales
blossom
enthroned.

The Gift of Pause

Inhale deeply and hold;
taste the flavor of your breath;
enfold it in memory of your tongue
to savor when you lose it.
Hesitate—

Feel the air around you;
stroke the comfort of an ordinary moment;
acknowledge the beauty of your skin,
your wrinkle, your sag, and all that drops away.
Attend—

Savor the noise of the street;
let it throb in your fingertips.
Listen to the pulse of your cat's purr,
and the comforting wheeze of the cushion as you sit.
Pause—

Draw in lampposts spilling puddles of amber
to relish when darkness comes
and madness overwhelms you
and the ordinary moments of contentment pass.
For what will come—
Rest.

Winter's Last Day

The sky foams in gray.
Tree branches, bony and bent,
finger the sky,
probing for something
just out of reach.

Glitter

The janitor said,
"No glitter,"
which they ignored,
and in their plum and pink prom dresses,
dusted themselves,
as young women will,
with gold and silver sparkle:
> It glowed on their arms at candle-lit tables.
> It shimmered in their hair,
> as they tossed their heads back laughing.
> It flickered on their toes,
> and lit a trail everywhere they danced.

And when midnight came
it still glistened
and shadowed them out the door
to pursue their dreams.
When someone said they couldn't
be a doctor-lawyer-singer-engineer,
their eyes sparked,
and they glittered a path of rebellion
until they owned
the hospital-court-stage-factory
and made it hum with light.

Their twinkling flickered
even in their homes
on graceful hands soothing a fevered child
or sifting sprinkles on birthday cakes,
so that children could learn
to light their own paths.

It dazzled lovers in Sunday morning embraces.
It seeped from pens in bright purple-y strokes
or oozed from fingers across keyboards.
Its brightness illuminated imaginations,
and gleamed in hearts,
flashing even in tears
of frustration and defeat.
It glinted brightly in anger
and outshone fears.

They lived defiantly,
and definitely,
and glowed all their lives.
And no dustpan-push-broom-wet-mop-wax
could wipe their burnished dust
from the tables-chairs-floors-boardrooms
or anywhere they went.
And they never heeded anyone
who told them:
"No glitter."

Graveyard Melodies

In the early chill of August dusk,
I stroll the local cemetery path
reading headstones—
summaries of lives I never knew.
With somber voices, those graveyard stones
darkly trill wayward hymns of memory.
Off-key, discordant,
in the thick-winged flutter of moths
hovering in faint light of faded dresses
and faltering shadows,
their cacophony tangles into symphony,
a recital of wraiths in an unfamiliar church yard.

Their serenade dredges up my dead,
resurrects them in their own sad songs.
I shroud them gently with simple melodies.
I tuck in ragged edges behind the sharps and pat them
rhythmically into soothing remembrance
small enough for a headstone—
a false lullaby humming
the way things never were.
In lilting carols, frayed history repairs.

Yet even as I do, my heart rebels,
and like some wild forest bird startles,
slips the chords, unravels its threads
and takes flight,
keening.

River Ride

A river is not water
but rock and reed and branch
and turn and bend, flowing,
gushing, spitting,
splashing clear,
tumbling in cloudy inches,
falling and rising
against landscape.
Moment glides to moment,
as we slide our silver paddles
to crease a wave, widen the arc,
turning—twisting in the water's flow.
We move in tandem
orchestrating our ride.
In silent conversations,
we grasp
at battered stones
or grind over gritty shallows.
Too casually, with a nod, a shrug
we chance an offshoot,
yearning for deep-water
and channeled currents
to cradle us.
Yet, with every rotation of wrist,
with each leaning of weight,
weariness overwhelms me, winds me,
chilling me in blankness—
unhinging me from the flow—
till I fear losing memory
of our ride,
this moment
where we breathed
and rocked against boulders,
trembling in our tinny haven,
knowing we were not river;
we were not fin or shell,
but other flesh and bone
rolling on our waves.

Kitties Kiss

Halloween moon glares
on a patent leather nose kissed wet
by a pink sandpaper tongue.

Deliberate Blindness

Mornings I roll from bed
—stagger to the kitchen.
    Knee-deep in winter snow,
      deer savor the bitter bark of backyard peach trees.
Car-loaded, seat-belted, prepared
I blurry-eye turn from our drive.
    Next door, in a window's glow, a silhouette
    achingly hunches over a bed, unable to straighten.
On the highway, I whiz by
weaving through truck and trailer.
    Numbed drivers, road-weary, sweaty, too-many-miles
    cramped, stare at the yellow-lined monotony, wilting.
A coffee-kicked-ten-minutes-energized later,
my world becomes a pinball game of warning lights and bleating horns.
    Sleep-deprived, a mother unbuckles at a stoplight,
    and turns to wipe a wheezing, feverish nose.
Parked, fully perked, intentional,
I juggle my rolling briefcase through the uncooperative doors
    A co-worker copying pulls papers; two sharp lines crease
    the space between eyes lost in some other world.
A sleepwalker, I am armored,
locked within my world
    protected, unbreached,
      sealed from the things I cannot—will not—must not—see.

Grandma's Icebox

One Sunday, we rode the bus to visit Grandma.
My father, stoic, sat buried in a *Free Press* crossword,
inking words effortlessly as the bus staggered forward.
In her aisle seat, across from Dad,
Mama gazed out the windshield,
restless in church clothes that never quite covered
her Southern drawl or Baptist roots
my Irish-Catholic grandmother despised.
My four-year-old self, warmed through my woolen coat
by my mother's soft side, pressed against the November window
breathing clouds and drawing pictures.

Factories and gritty streets chugged by.
At Kerchaval, we exited the bus then
picked our way over broken sidewalks,
past the worn brownstone facades,
careful of our step on the slippery, half-thawed patches,
until Grandma's house appeared, a chipped, bleak edifice.

Grandpa greeted us gruffly, his booming voice
so different from his taciturn son's.
In a spare bedroom, Mama laid our coats in a neat pile
while Grandpa backed into his overstuffed chair
pinned with stiff doilies, protection from the pomade
polishing his shiny black hair.
We lined the couch, perched in a pinched row, waiting.
Soon, Grandpa dug into his pockets
for the silver dollars he used to fish for me,
though he lured me more with smiles and open hands.

Grandma lingered in the kitchen chipping slivers
from a block of ice for the cool, dark drinks
she then offered us in fussy, etched glasses.
We sipped them, tongues numbing
under her chilly gaze in her wintry house,
where we shivered, even sweatered
in our heaviest clothes.

After, I carried my glass into the kitchen
where I could gaze on Grandma's icebox.
Like Grandma, her icebox was a short, wooden square,
with two compartments at heart:
in one was that block of ice,
hard and cool-blue clear as her Irish eyes.
The other never opened for me.

The bus ride home is endless—even today, I ride.
Just a glance in a mirror enfolds me in its sway—
I see my mother's smile and loose blonde waves,
my father's ink-smeared fingers,
and my grandfather's awkward, friendly reach.
Then grandmother's cool blue eyes pool back at me,
unthawed by time or place, undiminished cubes of ice
where her memory should be.

Night Lights

Night brews sun-steeped on a quiet eve:
    Gold sparkles through three-sistered windows,
    uncurtained, hung high on my bedroom wall.
    Cushioned in a favored chair, I lower
    my book, contemplating day,
    sorting memory like prayer beads.
Later, full-flushed silver freshens a breeze:
    under its cool sliver,
    I, unaudienced,
    choreograph my mood in playful steps
    and slide readied sheets
    to pillow in moonlight.
In tinseled night, I hand over my beads—
    payment for night solace;
    through the sisters, I listen
    as chimes dance the breeze,
    and in jeweled sleep
    I glide in remembrance.

Clive's Magic

Sunday evenings under a crisp of winter moon,
Clive made magic with bits of burger
fried in crushed garlic and oregano'd.
In a long tin, he latticed noodles and layered
slivered mozzarella crescents,
while we shuffled cards,
measuring our hopes in wistful bundles,
and recipe-d our tomorrows.

Later, he would spoon in his tomato-y
mix and oven it precisely
as we poured chilly apple ale,
in battered plastic glasses,
then tongued its
soothing sweet-yeasty sips
that mulled our anxious dreams
of acceptance letters
and sugar-salaried jobs.

In these intermissions,
of our cream-cheese-bagel-and-Taco–Bell-ed lives,
we whispered, longing for
what we had yet to taste,
and savored yearnings, the moonlit magic
of our winter feast,
as Clive spooned up
portions from his pan.

Some Dreams

Some dreams are dangerous:
They fog our paths,
cloak barriers, and haze our vision
with happy intentions.
Recklessly, they hijack us,
and, brakeless, run stoplights,
ram barricades
and ping-pong the curves.
Seductive sirens, they coo and entice
with sweet promises.
Like heart-pounding kisses,
they embroil us in passions—
deplete us, infect us,
then slither round our hearts,
wrapping themselves in
ever-tightening loops,
to squeeze us breathless.

Some dreams—
too dangerous
to ignore.

In Dreams

In dreams,
my husband's lover
locks him in ecstasy,
tangles him in legs and lips,
luring him from my arms;
yet in morning light
falling through backyard leaves—
through the kitchen window
where I stand,
bereft though wakened,
still tousled by imaginings—
I see him plant our garden.

I Didn't Get the Joke

I didn't get the joke
when they tripped him
stepping from the cafeteria line
toward his lonely table
and sloppy joe flew,
spewing the floor, and he, red faced,
gathered his thin bones
humiliated in the laughter
echoing in tinny air.

I didn't get the joke,
when they called her "Pizza-face"
and "Blubber-butt" and "Franken-fatty"
and she sank into herself in the second row,
hugging her books, eyes closed,
isolated in giggles,
muted behind sly fingers.

I didn't get the joke still
when the word came:
"Death by hanging," and the body floated
from a door, suspended by a belt,
pinned with a note,
and parents wept
while shocked laughter
reverberated in the hall.

Would someone
please
explain the "joke" to me?

Dregs of Winter

Grey-black snow mounds, the dregs of winter,
ripple brown-grassed curbs and dot parking lots
outside his window, where he peers, reluctant
to don his parka for the trek to school. He considers
his boots and gazes at the driveway's edge.
From their ashy ice, dead twigs and broken branches
spike their skeletal fingers, clawed and grasping.

Bootless, he joins three school-bound friends.
With them, he jostles on walkways patched with ice.
Sometimes, with ten-year-old glee,
they skid on the frost-plumped earth
balancing its glaze, arms spread like surfers.
In the pauses, though, his eyes skittle skyward
hoping for bits of blue;
mostly head bowed, he tracks
the ice-skimmed puddles of morning.
He tests one puddle's glass with his leather toes,
trying to drown whole the rigid plates
without soaking his socks.
If he could, he would drown winter, too,
and open the way to spring.
The ice crackles to spider webbing
and trickles seep the gaps,
freezing his sock in rigid wrinkles.

At the corner, where the boys turn
toward the school, he squeaks forward.
A willow shakes her new-gold leaves at them
when a bolt of sunlight daggers down her tresses—
blinding, painful, too brief. He sighs, wearied,
and hunches forward, bereft.

Winter, still jockeys the wind,
stinging.

Mary Fox is a Michigan native born in Detroit and raised in Warren, Michigan. She attended Lincoln High School, graduated, and enrolled in Michigan State University where she majored in English and earned her teaching degree. She later earned a Masters degree in education with an emphasis in writing from Central Michigan University. She taught literature and writing for 40 years at Fowler High School in Fowler, Michigan, and writing for 13 years at Lansing Community College. She also served as her local's union president and chief negotiator for several years. Widowed, she currently resides in Portland, Michigan, where she enjoys working with various political and charity groups, playing golf, swimming, spending days with family and friends, and of course, writing. She draws her inspiration from family memories and artifacts, experiences in the classroom, and observations of everyday life. Currently, she is developing her own blog site, working on short stories and a novel, and since she is also an active member of Writing at the Ledges in Grand Ledge, Michigan, she is contributing to and assisting in editing their fourth anthology of member works.

www.ingramcontent.com/pod-product-compliance
Lightning Source LLC
LaVergne TN
LVHW041518070426
835507LV00012B/1658